To

From

Date

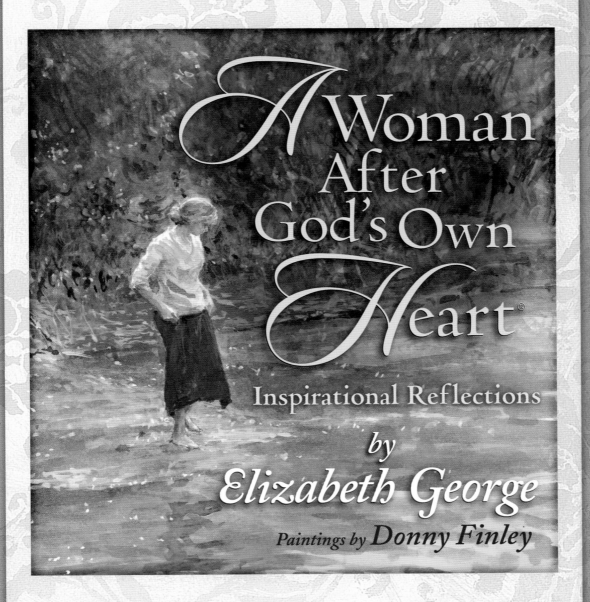

A Woman After God's Own Heart®

Inspirational Reflections

by

Elizabeth George

Paintings by Donny Finley

HARVEST HOUSE PUBLISHERS

EUGENE, OREGON

A Woman After God's Own Heart® Gift Edition

Text Copyright © 2010 by Elizabeth George

Published by Harvest House Publishers
Eugene, Oregon 97402
www.harvesthousepublishers.com

ISBN 978-0-7369-2559-4

Artwork copyright © Donny Finley

Design and production by Garborg Design Works, Savage, Minnesota

Scripture quotations are taken from the HOLY BIBLE, NEW INTERNATIONAL VERSION®. NIV®. Copyright © 1973, 1978, 1984 by the International Bible Society. Used by permission of Zondervan. All rights reserved. Some quotations are taken from The Message. Copyright © by Eugene H. Peterson 1993, 1994, 1995, 1996, 2000, 2001, 2002. Used by permission of NavPress Publishing Group.

Italicized text in Scripture quotations indicates author's emphasis.

Printed in Singapore

10 11 12 13 14 15 16 / IM / 10 9 8 7 6 5 4 3 2 1

CONTENTS

A Blessing
Dear Seeker of God's Heart,

It's wonderful being a woman after God's own heart, isn't it!

To know Him. To love Him. To enrich the lives of others.

To follow Him…and to take part in the blessings He extends to us.

No woman's life could be more satisfying than the life enjoyed

by a woman whose heart's desire is to do God's will. May God

richly bless you and yours as you continue to follow after Him.

In His everlasting love,

Elizabeth George

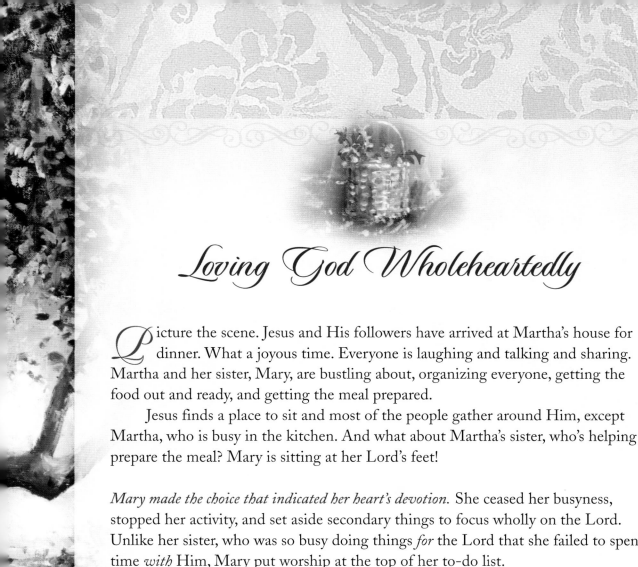

Loving God Wholeheartedly

*P*icture the scene. Jesus and His followers have arrived at Martha's house for dinner. What a joyous time. Everyone is laughing and talking and sharing. Martha and her sister, Mary, are bustling about, organizing everyone, getting the food out and ready, and getting the meal prepared.

Jesus finds a place to sit and most of the people gather around Him, except Martha, who is busy in the kitchen. And what about Martha's sister, who's helping prepare the meal? Mary is sitting at her Lord's feet!

Mary made the choice that indicated her heart's devotion. She ceased her busyness, stopped her activity, and set aside secondary things to focus wholly on the Lord. Unlike her sister, who was so busy doing things *for* the Lord that she failed to spend time *with* Him, Mary put worship at the top of her to-do list.

Mary chose the one thing needed. Because Mary was a woman after God's heart, she was preoccupied with one thing at all times—Jesus! Yes, she helped prepare the home for company, but when Jesus arrived, she dropped everything to spend time with Him. She knew nothing could take the place of time in His presence.

Time spent with Jesus fuels our lives and helps us focus on all we're called to do. He gives us energy and hope and love to deal with all the joyful and not-so-joyful events that occur during the day. As Jesus noted, time spent hearing and worshipping God can never be taken away! It provides permanent and everlasting dividends. As a woman who loves God, what choices can you make today to get to know Him better?

Choose God's ways at every opportunity. Every morning commit to choosing God and His ways in your decisions, words, thoughts, and responses today. How can you do this? Consider a two-step partnership with God:

- Your part is to stop and acknowledge God along the way.
- God's part is to direct your paths.

And when life gets hectic or difficult, take a brief second or two to talk to God. This doesn't mean the world comes to a grinding halt while you have a big discussion with God. You only have to mentally stop and check in with Him. That's acknowledging God, which is your part. Then wait for God to answer. He will, because that's His part.

Choose to focus on God when you can. When I lived in Los Angeles I spent a lot of time in the car. I used to listen to easy-listening music. Then it occurred to me that classical music would help me relax. This worked fine...until it occurred to me that I could be listening to Christian music that would lift my heart and mind to the Lord. Then I chose something even better! I chose CDs that taught biblical principles and listened to the Bible. Now I was learning more about God and His truths.

Then one day I turned the audio system off and landed on the best choice for my car time: memorizing Scripture.

Choose to stand in awe of God. A favorite passage of mine ends with these words: "Charm is deceptive and beauty is fleeting; but *a woman who fears the Lord* is to be praised" (Proverbs 31:30). Contemplate all that God has done for you and how He is directing your life. Pause to give Him thanks.

Choose to place your life and blessings in God's hands. Every morning, in a heartfelt prayer, start fresh with God by giving Him all that you are and all that you have. Lay everything on God's altar. Give Him your life, your body (such as it is), your health (or lack of it), your husband, each child (one by one), your home, your possessions, your job. Nurture the habit of placing these blessings in God's loving hands to do with them what He will.

Choose to have a passionate heart. Be on fire for the Lord. Let your life reflect your intense passion for Jesus. When a teakettle is boiling on the stove, it sputters and steams, it hops up and down and jiggles. Likewise let your love for God overflow, pouring out into your life…and into the lives of those around you. Speak often of what God has done for you.

Your Heart

Is your heart healthy and on fire for the Lord? Have you entered into an eternal relationship with God through His Son, Jesus? If you have, thank Him for the wonderful privilege of being called a child of God!

If you're unsure about where you stand with God or if you know you're living apart from Him, invite Jesus to be your Savior today. A simple prayer like this one from a sincere heart is all it takes:

God, I want to be Your child, a true woman after Your heart—a woman who lives her life in You, through You, and for You. I acknowledge my sin and receive Your Son, Jesus Christ, into my needy heart, giving thanks that He died for my sins.

Thank You for giving me Your strength so that I can follow You. Amen.

If you've responded to God's offer of a personal relationship with Him, welcome to God's family! If you know a Christian, call and share the good news. Ask around for a church where you can grow as a woman after God's own heart.

Eliminating Decision-making Stress

We're faced with myriad decisions every day. It's so easy to get bogged down and exhausted as we wonder what to do and when to do it. And if you're like me, some of your decisions haven't been the best. Perhaps you can relate to my experience.

The phone would ring around nine in the morning. A woman would ask me to speak at her church. Because I'd just eaten a scrambled egg and some toast, taken my thyroid pill, had a cup of coffee, and gone for a walk, I would be full of energy and blurt, "Sure! When do you want me to come?" At four in the afternoon, the phone would ring again. Another woman was calling with the same basic request, but because it was the end of a long day and I was beat and ready to relax, I would answer, "No way!" (My actual words were more gracious, but those were the words I was thinking.)

Why did I respond so differently? What criteria did I use for these decisions? In a word, *feelings*. While I was feeling full of fresh energy in the morning, my answer would be yes. In the late afternoon, when I was worn out, my answer would be no. My decisions were based on how I felt at the moment. I wasn't making decisions guided by God. I was making decisions based on my physical well-being.

The Impetus to Change

On my tenth birthday in the Lord, I was praising God for all He'd done for me. Then I asked Him if there was anything in my life He'd like me to focus on for the next "season" in my life. Prayer immediately came to my mind. Although I was an avid reader of the Bible and studied God's principles carefully, prayer had always been a weak area in my Christian walk.

I reached for a small book of blank pages that my daughter Katherine had given me. I hadn't quite known what to do with it, but suddenly I knew. Full of resolve, conviction, and desire, I wrote on the first page these words straight from my heart: "I dedicate and purpose to spend the next ten years (Lord willing) developing a meaningful prayer life."

This began an exciting leg on my spiritual journey. My commitment to prayer put into motion a complete makeover of my life. As I moved ahead, I was surprised by the blessings that blossomed in my heart. One of them was an incredible transformation in how I handled decisions.

A New Confidence

As I pursued a deeper prayer life, I soon developed a motto: *Make no decision without prayer.* I wrote down in my special little book every decision I needed to make. Whatever option arose, I asked for time to pray about it first. The more important the decision, the more time I asked for. If there wasn't time for me to pray about it, I generally answered no because I wanted to be sure my decisions were God's choices for me. I followed this approach for everything—invitations to showers, weddings, lunches, opportunities to minister, problems, ideas, crises, needs, even dreams. Every decision to make was written down and prayed about. What a difference it made! I avoided…

- becoming overcommitted and stressed
- people-pleasing
- making commitments I later had to back out of
- second-guessing my decisions
- activities that didn't use my God-given talents

Why not give this a try? I'm sure you'll see a huge difference in your life as you base your decisions on what God wants. Experience a new level of excitement for activities because you know you're doing what He wants you to! Remember: *Make no decision without prayer.*

Taming the Chaos

'd heard about many organizational solutions but never paid much attention. Standing in the supermarket checkout line, I'd invariably see some magazine promising tips that would end my time-management problems once and for all. And as a voracious reader I'd spent a lot of time in bookstores and noticed rows of books on getting life under control. But for a long time I had zero motivation in this area.

Then one day as I studied God's Word, something jumped out at me that changed my attitude. What was it? It was God's tip, God's solution! It was a verse that advises women like me to "guide the house"—to manage, love, and take care of my home (1 Timothy 5:14).

Furthermore, the why of this statement was clear. Evidently some women were wandering around gossiping and being busybodies. Their negative behavior and lack of discipline were causing some people to speak poorly of Christianity.

This message found a place in my heart! I was certainly idle at times and guilty of a few not-so-great habits. I knew I needed to take action. But first, to be sure I was headed in the right direction, I wanted to get a handle on the meaning of the word *guide* in this verse.

I found out that the woman who manages her house is the home manager. I learned that every day we're called to manage what God has given us, to use our resources to the best of our ability for our good and to further God's purposes.

How does a woman who wants what God wants, a woman who wants to know order instead of chaos, a woman after God's own heart, manage her home?

Understand that home management is God's best for us. God isn't asking His women to *like* being a home manager (although that comes with time as we reap the blessings of better home management). And God isn't asking us to *feel like* managing our home. He's simply asking us to do it.

Take home management seriously. How well we keep our homes has a gigantic impact on our families. As women, we usually establish the home atmosphere. We want to provide a positive, safe, and comfortable environment so our family and friends can relax, recover from the stresses of the day, and have fun. And we need these things too!

God also uses the management of our homes as a training ground for usefulness in the body of Christ, our community, and the world at large. How effectively we manage the home often indicates how well we'll manage outside interests. For example, if we're good stewards of the responsibilities at home, we'll probably be good stewards of the resources in an organization. Jesus said, "He who is faithful in what is least is faithful also in much" (Luke 16:10).

If we have jobs that generate income, we can be more focused on our work because the people at home are cared for and everything is somewhat under control. And as we tame the chaos at home, we have more time to pursue ministries and activities that benefit others.

One tool that really helped me get organized was developing a schedule. On specific days I planned housework, errands, and time with friends. I scheduled time with my husband, Jim, for special activities together. The same went for our daughters. I also worked in some kind of involvement at church and did part time bookkeeping at home. Order emerged out of chaos when I scheduled what was important.

Care about the condition of your home and the use of your time. When our family and guests walk into our homes and look around, they get a sense of our priorities and how well we're doing in response to God's call to manage our homes. What do people see when they enter your house? Do they find calm or chaos? Peace or panic? Organization or a mess? Is God honored in your home, by the condition of your home, and by your lifestyle at home?

Time Management Simplified

In my efforts to become better organized and more effective, I've learned some principles that helped me…and will help you get your time under control.

1. *Plan in detail*—Have a planner and write everything down. The more you plan, the better you manage and the more you achieve. The more detailed your plans are, the better. Try planning twice a day—last thing at night and first thing in the morning.

2. *Deal with today*—All God asks of you is that you handle and manage today. Don't worry about tomorrow or stress about yesterday. Each day is an opportunity to start fresh and be successful. Jesus said, "Do not worry about tomorrow, for tomorrow will worry about its own things. Sufficient for the day is its own trouble" (Matthew 6:34).

3. *Value each minute*—Know how long it takes to complete the tasks in your home. Are you facing a 2-minute task or a 20-minute one? Then decide if the task is the best use of the time. You'll also be able to squeeze in tasks when you have a few minutes while waiting for the clothes to dry, dinner to cook, or during commercials when you're watching TV.

4. *Keep moving*—Remember the principle of momentum: "A body at rest [human or otherwise] tends to remain at rest, and a body in motion tends to remain in motion." Tell yourself, "Just one more thing…just five more minutes." Keep moving and you can cross one more thing off your to-do list.

5. *Develop a routine*—Doing the same thing at the same time each day conserves energy by cutting down on indecision. You perform menial tasks by rote. It also generates energy because you know what needs to be done and when, and plan accordingly. Put as many tasks as possible into your routine.

6. *Exercise and diet*—Exercise increases metabolism, creates energy, helps you be more rested, and produces pleasure hormones that contribute to positive attitudes, joy in life, and a general lust for life. The word *diet* simply means "a way of life," so develop a healthy way of eating that gives the people in your household the best life possible.

7. *Ask the "half the time" question*—"If my life depended on doing this task in half the time I've allotted, what shortcuts would I take?" Then take them.

8. *Use a timer*—Setting the timer for "just five minutes" can get you started. Setting the timer for "I'll quit in five minutes" can keep you going. Also, when you set the timer, try to beat the clock. There's something motivating about hearing time tick away.

9. *Do the worst first*—What is the worst task on your to-do list? Do it first to avoid a heavy cloud of dread hanging over you all day. Once the worst is done, your attitude will be greatly improved and you'll have more energy for the remaining tasks.

10. *Read daily on time management*—Just five minutes a day will help you discover new ideas and methods that can make your life a lot easier and more effective.

11. *Say no*—Make your daily schedule and call it "Plan A." Follow your plan by saying no to other activities that come along. Be flexible though, in case God calls you to a "Plan B," such as an unexpected opportunity to help someone.

12. *Begin the night before*—Get a jump on tomorrow by implementing these suggestions the night before:

- Plan the next day
- Plan the next day's meals
- Select, lay out, and prepare clothes
- Clean up the kitchen
- Run the dishwasher
- Set the table for the next meal
- Tidy up the house
- Prepare lunches and meals
- Sort the wash and get a load going in the washer
- Put things you need to take with you by the door
- At your office, take the last 10 minutes of the workday to make a to-do list and gather phone numbers, papers, and other items you'll need for your first project in the morning.

Little steps like these can bring great results! And once you get started, you'll find energy and enthusiasm to keep you moving. One last tip: Ask God to help you move toward better management. Consult Him often during the day. He cares about everything you do...and He loves you!

Reaching Out to Help

For Thanksgiving one year, our family gathered in Maui, where my newlywed daughter had moved. We had a wonderful holiday filled with laughter, love, and liveliness. On one of our sightseeing excursions we traveled 30 miles on an exhausting, carsick-producing road that snaked around hills and through valleys. At the end we came to a breathtaking view of the Seven Sacred Pools.

High up in the mountains, the ever-present rain clouds unleashed fresh water that rushed down the mountainsides and filled the highest pool. When that pool was full, the water overflowed into a second pool. It continued to cascade down through five more pools until the last and final pool poured its contents into the immensity of the Pacific Ocean.

As I stood with my family marveling at this wondrous handiwork of God, I thought of the life you and I seek to live as God's women. These seven pools illustrate the fullness we can enjoy—and the far-reaching impact we can have—as we live and love according to God's plan.

Picture again that top pool, high on that mountain, veiled in a cloudy mist, hidden from the sight of others. Like that pool, you and I enjoy our hidden life with God, the private life we nurture in Him and with Him in private. Unseen by others, we are filled by God's Spirit as we dwell in His presence and drink from His Word. In that holy mist

He replenishes our dry souls until we're filled with His goodness. Then that fullness overflows down into the next pool, the hearts of the people nearest and dearest to us.

Then it happens again. Still high on the mountain, out of our fullness, God grows in us a servant spirit and a heart filled with love. This pool of love swells until it cascades into the lives of extended family and close friends.

The bounteous richness of our relationships with God, family, and friends splashes into the next pool, filling our homes with God's love, family, and intimate friends. The springs of God's love and care flow into the lives of our spiritual family—the people in our church.

And then the water overflows again to the next levels, satisfying our soul's desires and filling the lagoon where dreams are dreamed and we get a glimpse of what God wants us to do for Him and His people. We submerge ourselves in this fresh pool of knowledge, discipline, and training until the water level rises to the brink and surges beyond, pouring out God's limitless ocean of ministry and service that builds His people up.

From our vantage point, as we reflect on how God might use us, we are silenced, awestruck. Now we understand! His ways are wise, and His ways work. When we are faithful to follow after God's heart—when we tend and nurture each aspect of life as He instructs—the ministry He uses us in can have an impact beyond measure.

As the fresh rain of God's love fills your pools and overflows, how can you direct the flow into the lives of others?

Giving

Again and again Jesus tells us to give—to give to everyone in the generous way God gives. What are some easy ways to reach out to people?

Be available. Your presence and touch are worth a thousand words. When it comes to reaching out, your very presence is a source of comfort. Especially with today's hectic schedules, taking the time to be with someone can be a huge blessing for both of you. You may not know the exact words to say or the perfect Scripture to share, but a quick touch and time together can bring comfort greater than words.

Be a giver. Offer a smile, a cheerful greeting, a caring question, a loving touch, and a quick hug. Always address the person by name. As an added bonus, include a sincere compliment or share one of the reasons you like your friend.

Be generous. Don't just give, but give liberally, cheerfully, and bountifully. Proverbs 11:25 informs us "The one who blesses others is abundantly blessed; those who help others are helped." Over the decades I've tried to grow in the grace of giving. At one point I put developing a more giving heart on my prayer list. I pursued this Christlike character quality and regularly asked God, "Who can I give to today? Who's in need? Show me." And you don't have to have wealth to give. You have groceries in the pantry, clothes and maybe even baby items someone else can use, books that encourage and edify, your time, your love, your support. You can offer sincere praise, encouragement, thanks, a greeting, kindness, and notes of appreciation.

Be direct. When you see a person in need, be direct. Walk up to the person and see what he or she needs and figure out what you can do to help. Don't hope someone else will come along. And don't go looking for someone else to help. God has allowed *you* to find this person in need. Let your heart overflow with care.

Be bold. If you're shy, step out in faith to give, and God will give you the courage. Don't hesitate to offer a warm, friendly greeting to people you meet. Reach out to someone every day. Let Christ in you shine.

What a privilege God gives us…that we can give others joy by simply giving generously.

Encouraging Others

One Sunday my husband, Jim, was teaching on reaching out to others. He said something I've never forgotten: "With every encounter, make it your aim that people are better off for having been in your presence. Try in every encounter to give something to the other person." What a great—and simple—way to positively influence the lives of other people!

In a section on encouraging others, you might be expecting a list of what you can do for others. However, to effectively give support and encouragement to others, we need to be filled with God's love and compassion. What can we do to prepare to uplift others?

Take time to be filled. The most important preparation for a ministry of encouragement is to spend time with Jesus. You need to commune with Him often to be replenished. Studying God's Word and allowing the Holy Spirit to fill us provides never-ending support, strength, and wisdom. God's fullness in us will overflow into the lives of others.

Develop skills and overcome weaknesses. Service to others is increased when you take the time to develop your skills and overcome your weaknesses. Doesn't that make sense?

How much can a teacher teach, a counselor counsel, an administrator administrate if they haven't learned the necessary skills? As you grow in Christ, you'll find the power and knowledge for overcoming personal weaknesses and develop ways to be more effective in reaching and blessing others in Jesus Christ.

Memorize Scriptures of encouragement. It's difficult to give away what you don't possess. So why not memorize Scripture verses of encouragement to share with people in need? Knowing God's wisdom will help you offer uplifting encouragement that is timely and appropriate to the situation. That way you'll have the knowledge you need ready for any situation!

If you are faithful to memorize gems from God's Word, you'll suddenly find them adding real substance to your conversations. This is another natural overflow from a heart full of God's love. You'll find the content of the notes you write and the phone calls you make taking on added depth. Your visits with others will become more meaningful as you share God's powerful truths and promises. In fact, because your heart is full of Scripture, you'll no longer be satisfied with meaningless, trivial conversations. Sharing God's Word will take your talks with others to deeper levels.

Call someone. "Worry weighs us down; a cheerful word picks us up" (Proverbs 12:25). You probably know this from experience. An easy way to encourage and make a heart glad is to contact people by phone. I'm not talking about calling long lists of people or talking to someone for 30 minutes or more. A simple, quick call can do much to gladden a person's heart. A familiar voice from someone who loves him or her can make the day special.

I usually make these "sunshine calls" in the afternoon. I pray before I dial to be positive, energetic, uplifting. I ask God to give me the words to build up the people I'm calling, compliment them, remind them of their strengths, let them know how proud I am of them…and always express my respect for who they are and what they do. When the people I call answer, the first thing I ask is, "Is this a good time to talk or would you like me to call you back?" And if they don't answer the phone, I leave a cheerful message that I'm thinking about them and hope to call again soon. I don't ask them to call me back. I've witnessed how hectic life can get, and they don't need one more thing on their to-do lists.

When I call I say something like, "I know you're about to eat—and so are we, but I haven't seen you lately so I just wanted to give you a quick call to make sure everything is going well." If there is a difficulty, I make an appointment to call back at a time when we can have a more lengthy and meaningful conversation. You can also reach out in this way to people recovering from illnesses or dealing with a crisis. The telephone is a very effective way to encourage others, and it takes very little effort. Most important to encouraging others is a heart that cares! Who can you share a smile with by phone?

Write notes or emails of encouragement. Writing notes to those who need encouragement is another great way to share a good word that makes the heart glad. You want to convey to people that you care and are available if they need you.

The people I admire most in this area of note writing are those who set aside certain time slots in their day or week for the purpose of writing notes and letters. It *is* a ministry! And if you're thinking, "I'm already so busy. How can I add one more thing?" consider my simple approach. As I face a blank piece of notepaper, I tell myself, "Come on, Elizabeth, this person's need is important. Just three sentences. You can do it!" Whether I'm writing to the sick, the bereaved, those in leadership, or a recent hostess, telling myself "Just three sentences!" gets me going.

- Sentence #1 conveys I miss you, I appreciate you, I'm thinking of you.
- Sentence #2 lets readers know they are special to me and why.
- And sentence #3 says I'm praying for them and includes the actual verse I'm praying for them.

As you sit in bed or on a couch with your feet propped up, you can give this kind of encouragement to others out of your heart and the recipients will be very blessed!

Everywhere I go I carry a folder that contains correspondence I need to answer, the names of those I need to thank, and a supply of note cards, envelopes, postcards, and stamps. I also carry my laptop computer so wherever I am—on a plane, in a hotel, at an airport, waiting for my husband in the car, or sitting in a coffee shop—I can encourage others with a note. And so can you—in just three sentences!

Serving and being a blessing to others is always a matter of the heart. If your heart is filled with a watchful concern for God's people, you will be privileged to refresh many souls in need of encouragement just like rain clouds deliver much-needed moisture to a parched earth.

Growing Joy

Are you happy? Do you feel like your life is fulfilling and successful? Two sure ways to find joy is to develop your personal relationship with Christ and to be actively using the gifts God has given you. How and what you do—whether in ministry, in a career, within your family, or in other activities—will reflect your faith in Christ. The apostle Paul said, "Whatever you do, work at it with all your heart, as working for the Lord" (Colossians 3:23). God wants you to pursue Him and everything you do with a spirit of excellence and joy.

On Fire!

One Sunday morning I stopped to talk to a long-time acquaintance. As Sharon talked that morning, she seemed electric—lit up, sparks flying, flowing and sizzling with live juice. Everything about her evidenced her wholehearted pursuit of continued growth in her Savior, Jesus Christ. Her brilliant smile and bright eyes sparkled with energy as she punctuated her message with excited gestures and waves.

What was she on fire about? Sharon was looking forward to hearing a very special speaker the next day. She could hardly wait! Her words tumbled out as she explained who the scholar was and what she was already learning. As she talked, I knew I was in the presence of a woman who was growing in the knowledge and love of her Lord. No wonder she was so happy and excited! No wonder she had so much to give to others. No wonder I felt blessed by her.

Can you sense how stimulating Sharon was? Can you see why she spurs me on in my spiritual growth? This woman after God's own heart is vibrant. There's an infectiousness about her life and heart that challenges and motivates. It's impossible to leave her presence unchanged. Her joy shines, and everyone who gets close receives something from the fullness of her life. It's obvious she's doing what she loves to do and what she's been gifted to do.

My deepest desire and prayer for you and me is that we will become this kind of woman! I'm sure you're familiar with the saying, "When nothing is coming in, nothing can go out." So to be effective in life and to be successful, step one is to be filled with God, so He can use us to reach others for Him.

Discipleship

Spiritual growth, as with anything we want to grow in, is an investment of your time and hearts. God's ideal for us is that we learn and then teach others the good things we've discovered. We usually equate this discipleship with one-on-one meetings with someone over a long time period. That would be wonderful, but for most people it's neither a reality nor a possibility. However, there are enriching alternatives for growth—spiritual and other—as long as we bear in mind that God wants us to bear good fruit for Him in everything we do.

Classes are available. Churches offer Bible studies and Bible classes. Correspondence courses are available from Bible colleges and seminaries. Community classes also offer a wide variety of good topics to pursue.

Books offer another avenue for growth and help you develop skills for helping others. To speed up your growth, read and work through growth and study guide workbooks.

Counsel from fellow Christians is also a valid form of discipleship. If you have a problem, you can ask a trusted and godly person—and you'll receive God's perspective and the prayer support you need. Even if you're unable to attend any classes or meet with a mentor right now, you can always ask for counsel.

Interviewing is one of my favorite means of growth and discipleship. When God sent a godly, older woman to my church, I took one look at her busy life and saw clearly that she wouldn't have time to meet with me regularly. So I made a list of questions I wanted to ask and set up an appointment. We met one time, but those two precious hours were life changing! Much of my philosophy of helping people and many of the things I teach are a result of that blessed time I spent drinking in her wisdom.

Observation is another great way to grow. Bible teacher Carole Mayhall says one way to learn how to love and demonstrate respect and support for our spouses is to watch other women. Carole says, "Keep a list of how other women show admiration for their husbands. Watch, learn, write down what you learn, and then try those new behaviors yourself." And this works for raising children, helping family members, assisting elderly parents, and working with people in all types of situations.

Reading plays an important role in spiritual growth. The main book to read is your Bible, of course. Then you can read books by people who love the Lord. Are you thinking, *But I don't have time to read!* Carrying a book everywhere allows you to read while waiting at doctors' offices, in line at the post office, and other waiting times. I used to set my timer and read for five minutes a day. It doesn't sound like much, but that approach gets many books read! Another great source are Christian magazines. Their articles are short and packed with information for growing your faith and serving others.

Goals

I can't imagine life without goals. Goals give me a target. As I get up each morning and take aim at my day, the arrow I shoot may wobble and weave, but at least it's in flight and headed somewhere. The arrow may miss the bull's-eye, fall a little short, or sometimes go quite wide of the goal. But at least it was going—*I* was going—somewhere. Goals are definitely a good thing when it comes to spiritual growth.

Goals provide focus. If you aim at nothing, you'll hit it every time. When I was a mom with preschoolers, I aimed at reading one book a year. My first book was Edith Schaeffer's *What Is a Family?* It helped me determine the road I wanted our family to head down. I read it in

bits and pieces, remembering that *something is better than nothing*. I set a goal—and reached it. Through the years I've read many great books that have helped my growth and my ability to help others.

Goals provide opportunities for specific measurement. Setting goals that are specific helps you move in the direction you want to go. When it comes to goals, stay away from the vague. The goal "to be a godly woman" or "to walk with God" is honorable but hard to measure. It's far better to be specific. Ask "What does a godly woman *do*?" and let your answer give specific and measurable behaviors (Bible study, prayer time, helping others). Then write down steps you can take toward those behaviors and mark them off as you accomplish them.

Goals provide encouragement. When a week, or month, or year is over, do you ever wonder, *Wow, what did I do? Where did it go?* By writing down specific, measurable goals and keeping track of my progress in my planner, I can see where growth has taken place, the number of books I've read, the variety of classes and seminars I've taken or taught, the audiences I've shared God's truths with, the books I've written, and the number of family reunions and birthdays celebrated. Tracking your efforts and God's grace let's you celebrate your progress and give God thanks.

Once you've settled on specific goals, you have to continually make choices that support them. You can choose to study your Bible instead of going to the mall. You can choose to spend time in prayer instead of meeting friends for lunch. You can choose to give up espressos to contribute money to a local food bank.

God will honor the time you commit to learning more about Him, growing in Him, and doing good works in His name. An image from Scripture I love encourages me. The prophet Isaiah wrote, "Those who hope in the Lord will renew their strength. They will soar on wings like eagles" (Isaiah 40:31). The time you spend in solitude with your Bible and your prayer lists is time spent waiting and hoping in the Lord. Then, in the fullness of God's perfect timing, you take flight like an eagle. You are able to soar because you've been with the Lord.

When the timing is right, when the opportunity for ministry presents itself, you will soar like eagles because you're ready to do God's work! Then live out the saying that "success comes when preparation meets opportunity." God is responsible for presenting the opportunities—in His time, place, and manner—but you are responsible for cooperating with His efforts to prepare you.

Experiencing Joy

Picture a real woman you admire. Most likely she's stimulating, challenging, energetic, and joyful. She's growing and fresh, excited and exciting, learning and willing to share what she's learning. She motivates you, and you love to be in her presence.

Such a woman is probably involved in and committed to spiritual growth. She's spent time with God and been filled by Him so she's compelled to share her love for Jesus. She reveals the joys of knowing Him and walking with Him. He's filled her heart to overflowing, enabling her to offer refreshment to other people.

As you watch her dip into the reservoir created by her time with God and as you listen to her enthusiasm for life and for the Lord, you realize you're in the presence of a woman who truly knows God's joy and has responded to His call. And you'll be even more blessed if you accept the invitation to do likewise! So take a moment and wait on the Lord as you consider these life-changing questions:

- How am I spending my God-given time and energy?
- Am I wasting time on choices that have no heavenly value?
- Do I realize the value of time spent in preparation with the Lord?
- Have I set aside time to spend with God and be in His Word so I can be prepared to help others and serve Him?
- Am I letting time slip away unused, wasted, or not reaching my full potential?

God has saved us, given us eternal life, blessed us, gifted us for ministry, and prepared a place for us in heaven. And now He calls on us to...

- catch His vision
- make growth in Him a goal
- spend time with Him preparing to reach out to others
- trust Him to provide opportunities to help people
- reach out with His love and in His name

Praise Him now and commit yourself again to being a woman after God's own heart.

A Closing Prayer

May I live a life worthy of You. May I please You in every way. May I bear fruit in every good work, grow in the knowledge of You, be strengthened with all power according to Your glorious might so that I may have great endurance and patience, and joyfully give thanks to You, the Father, who makes it possible for me to share in the inheritance of the saints in the kingdom of light. Amen.